THE WORLDS OF ARCHITECTURAL DIGEST

HISTORIC INTERIORS

THE WORLDS OF ARCHITECTURAL DIGEST

HISTORIC INTERIORS

EDITED BY PAIGE RENSE

EDITOR-IN-CHIEF, ARCHITECTURAL DIGEST

THE KNAPP PRESS   PUBLISHERS   LOS ANGELES

THE VIKING PRESS   DISTRIBUTORS   NEW YORK

Published in the United States of America in 1979
The Knapp Press
5900 Wilshire Boulevard, Los Angeles, California 90036
Copyright © 1979 by Knapp Communications Corporation
All rights reserved
First Edition

Distributed by The Viking Press
625 Madison Avenue, New York, New York 10022

Distributed simultaneously in Canada by Penguin Books Canada Limited

Library of Congress Cataloging in Publication Data
Main entry under title: Historic interiors.
(The Worlds of Architectural digest)
Selections from the pages of Architectural digest, newly edited and designed.
1. Interior decoration — History. 2. Historic Buildings.
I. Rense, Paige. II. Architectural digest. III. Series.
NK1710.H57   1979   747'.8'8   77-84683

ISBN 0-89535-033-5
Printed and bound in the United States of America

CONTENTS

FOREWORD

The houses I have selected for inclusion in this particular volume, all adapted and revised from past issues of ARCHITECTURAL DIGEST, are historical. Most of them are houses where some notable figure of the past actually lived, and in the majority of cases nothing has been done to change the original décor. The fact that few changes have been made seems to me one of the most attractive elements of this kind of feature—a feature that has always been popular with our readers.

For those who are interested in history, and in the history of interior design, there is no more pleasant way to recapture the past than visually. Everything else aside, there is an undeniable emotional impact in being able to see, almost exactly as it was at the time, Winston Churchill's studio, for example, or D'Annunzio's writing desk or the bedroom of Marie Antoinette at Versailles.

In such a way historical personages, and history itself, come to life with a vividness that is nearly impossible to create by the written word alone. The written word is here, of course, and it does serve to amplify and explain. But I feel one of the major attractions of ARCHITECTURAL DIGEST—and something I have always tried to emphasize—is the visual unfolding of the way in which people live, the way in which they have created unique and personal environments for themselves. In modern-day apartments and houses, of course, much of the décor has been arranged with the help of professional interior designers. This is not generally the case with the historic houses to be found in this particular volume. Each has the stamp of a single personality upon it. Each shows how a particular individual, more often than not a well-known historical figure, has expressed his or her personality in various eras and in various parts of the world.

Not all of these houses, I am sure, are to every taste, but they do form a unique record of the past—an authentic past, in no way conjured up by professionals. Do not misunderstand. I have nothing but admiration for the fine work interior designers have done in the field of traditional design. But here we are dealing with an entirely different subject matter. We are dealing literally with the past, and to this end I have tried to make an appealing selection of the many interesting, unusual and provocative historical houses that have appeared over the years in ARCHITECTURAL DIGEST.

Today, more than ever, I think there is a particular relevance in the study and consideration of history. Many people now are inclined to overlook the past—unless in the context of a certain narcissistic nostalgia—and to find no particular meaning in it. We seem to have become a generation overwhelmingly, and perhaps unhappily, concerned only with the present moment. It is easy for us to forget that Peter Paul Rubens and Washington Irving were quite as concerned with their own particular moments. And these particular moments of the past are what I am asking you to look at in the pages that follow. I know you will share some of the excitement and interest that I have shared with my editors, photographers and writers in bringing these treasures of history to your attention.

Paige Rense
Editor-in-Chief
Los Angeles, California

THE WORLDS OF ARCHITECTURAL DIGEST

HISTORIC INTERIORS

THE
PETER PAUL RUBENS
HOUSE

The house of Peter Paul Rubens in Antwerp, now preserved as a museum, is an architectural statement as well, giving insight into the painter's style. Flemish conservatism and the then avant-garde Italian classicism are mixed in the design of the house, as in the style of the famous artist who built it.

The paintings of Rubens are characterized by a classicism rendered with a distinctive sense of realism that evolves from the tradition seen also in the work of van Eyck and Memling. In the structure itself this traditionalism is expressed in the Medieval and functional use of plain brick, exposed beams, simple wainscoting and large windows. Italian elements, such as ambitious decorative pediments and niches, are unexpected notes of elegance. In fifteenth-century Italy, during the early Renaissance, simpler functional architecture was being replaced; in Flanders it never went completely out of style. Rubens, however, used the Renaissance as the point of departure for his own innovative style.

The house today is the result of a restoration that was begun in 1938, a year after the city of Antwerp acquired it. There had been a number of changes made since Rubens's death in 1640. One of the early occupants, the duke of Newcastle, operated a stylish riding academy on the grounds while he was a refugee in Antwerp. An engraving of the building in 1684 suggests the drastic changes that followed. The engraving was helpful to the restorers, who were able to confirm architectural details of the house as Rubens knew it. Digging, scraping and studying fragments of the original complex helped the restorers determine the decorative treatment of many of the rooms. The restoration took about eight years, some of them during World War II, when the restoration became a symbol of hope for the future. The house finally opened as a museum in 1946.

Peter Paul Rubens acquired the property and the original house in 1610, when he was thirty-three and already a successful artist. Long a resident of Italy, where he had been in the employ of the duke of Mantua, he returned to Antwerp when his mother died. Before long he fell in love, married and settled down with his bride, Isabella Brandt. It took at least six years to transform the site into the home Rubens envisioned for himself. Documents of the time suggest it took even longer for him to pay for the project. The interior and the exterior both reveal the balancing of traditionalism and classicism. Inside, fine locally made furniture was the background for an art collection that Rubens gathered, which included decorative objects, ancient sculpture and various artworks of his own era. All were arranged in a comfortable, partly old-fashioned, rambling house that, however, had a number of distinguishing features.

The courtyard is a trenchant example of the general style of the house. The stone is handled in a way that reveals a knowledge of the advanced design of the period, and the overall look is most elaborate. Originally the upper stories of this façade were painted, but to make the restoration more durable relief decorations were substituted. The lower story has always had a series of niches to house classical busts. The garden façade is in higher relief, with the niches deeper and occupied by allegorical figures. Thus the painter's house offers a dramatic contrast between the period's conservative and advanced approaches to design. Many of the rooms are simple, with beamed ceilings and plaster walls, but there are also richly carved fireplaces and other touches of elegance. The excitement of the Rubens house today is the stunning bridge it provides between functionalism and elaboration in the context of early-seventeenth-century Antwerp.

Seventeenth-century master painter Peter Paul Rubens acquired his Antwerp studio/residence in 1610 and spent years transforming it to satisfy his exacting cosmopolitan tastes. Restored between 1938 and 1946, it is a refined amalgam of functional Flemish traditionalism and Italian classicism that mirrors the artist's grand vision. PRECEDING PAGE: Arched windows, sculpture-filled niches and applied sculptures are among the Baroque architectural features that enrich the studio's Courtyard façade. A portico connects the studio and residential wings. RIGHT: Seen from the street, the house is reminiscent of an Italian palazzo.

OPPOSITE BOTTOM: *At one end of the stone-paved Courtyard, an elaborate arcade surmounted by urns and free-standing sculptures encloses the U-shaped structure. Beyond it is a charming garden in the Italian style.* LEFT: *A view from the garden reveals the back of the studio and of the adjacent arcade. At right is the simpler brick residential wing, with gables and Flemish-style double windows.* BELOW: *The Portico that connects the residence and studio is open to the elements. Counterpointing the severe geometry of its checkered tile floor are an ornate coffered ceiling and a classical balustrade.*

LEFT: *In the residential wing, the Living Room's beamed ceiling, plaster walls and tall windows are examples of Flemish architecture. A painting by Rubens's contemporary, Adam van Noort, hangs above the mantel.*
BELOW LEFT: *Earthenware Antwerp tiles and a traditional chimney cloth adorn the fireplace in the Dining Room. Walls are enriched by tooled leather, and a Rubens self-portrait.*

TOP: *Jacob van Utrecht's 1530 portrait of Rubens's grandmother hangs in the living room.* ABOVE: *A window in the residential wing overlooks courtyard and studio.* OPPOSITE: *The 17th-century Flemish Kitchen resembles a Northern Renaissance genre painting.*

14

RIGHT: *The Bedroom where Rubens died exhibits typical 17th-century Flemish features: a brass chandelier, an embroidered chimney cloth, a carpet-covered table and small leaded-glass window panes. Equally representative is the light-to-dark contrast of pale walls and rich, deep-toned wood.* BELOW RIGHT: *Another Bedroom contains Jan van Boekhorst's portrait of Rubens's second wife, Hélène Fourment, and a 17th-century Antwerp-crafted bed.* OPPOSITE: *Rubens housed his extensive art collection in this Gallery. In his day, it may have resembled the painting by Willem van Hacht depicting an art collection assembled by one of Rubens's patrons. Italianate marble architectural detailing distinguishes the adjacent apsidal gallery filled with Greco-Roman antiquities.*

SAGAMORE HILL

It sits proudly on the spine of a hill ringed by dogwood, oak and hickory near Cove Neck on Long Island's gracious North Shore, overlooking Oyster Bay and Long Island Sound. *Sagamore Hill* is as striking today as when it was the summer White House and home of Theodore Roosevelt, one of America's most colorful presidents. Here pomp and circumstance were traded for the happy laughter and boisterous activities of the president and his six children. A devoted husband and loving father, he wanted the children to have lasting memories of the home they grew up in, as he did.

"Fond as I am of the White House and much though I have appreciated these years in it," he wrote to one of his children, "there isn't any place in the world like home—like Sagamore Hill, where things are our own, with our own associations." It was the kind of high-spirited place where houseguests on arrival were not allowed to unpack, but rather urged to get into their bathing costumes or riding clothes; where dogs and children—as many as sixteen Roosevelt cousins at once—ran, uninhibited, among the foreign dignitaries and heads of state; where an ordinary sight would be the president rowing energetically on the bay or jumping off the barn roof with his children.

As a boy Roosevelt had summered with his family in the same Oyster Bay area and had fallen in love with the Sound, the open meadows, the rolling hills and the bird and plant life. Two months after his first marriage, in 1880, he purchased one hundred fifty-five acres and made plans with the architectural firm of Lamb and Rich to build a house that would express "solidity, dignity, hospitality, comfort and permanence." It was to be a home for his wife and their expected child. In 1884, however, shortly before construction plans were completed, his wife,

Alice, died in childbirth, on the same day his mother died. A desolate T.R. went west to a ranch in the Badlands, but before leaving he arranged to have the home built for his baby. It was completed in early 1885, and there he brought his child and his new wife, the former Edith Carow. Mrs. Roosevelt lived at Sagamore Hill until her death in 1948, nearly thirty years after that of her husband. The house was then purchased by the Theodore Roosevelt Association, which presented it to the United States Government in 1963 as a national monument.

Very nineteenth-century in mood, Sagamore Hill's interiors are inclined to be a mass of Victorian clutter and dark wood with the unexpected additions of Roosevelt's hunting trophies: stuffed animal heads, fur rugs, skins and horns. In general, however, the Roosevelts seemed more concerned with who was in their house than what it contained. They loved entertaining. Luncheons, teas, dinners and any number of houseguests were all part of the normal Sagamore Hill routine.

As the family expanded and the social obligations of the presidency mounted, the North Room was added in 1905. Designed by C. Grant LaFarge, it was, to Theodore Roosevelt's tastes, "the most attractive feature of my house." Thirty feet wide by forty feet deep, with a high vaulted ceiling, the North Room features black walnut columns set in pairs against all four walls and a variety of woods — mahogany, swamp cypress and hazel—that contribute to the room's special and personal quality. Hanging jauntily, as if they were put there only yesterday, are T.R.'s well-known upturned hat, sword and binoculars, dating from his Rough Rider days in Cuba. Indeed, little about Sagamore Hill seems to have changed, and it is easy today to sense the magic and vitality of those vanished years.

Sagamore Hill was Theodore Roosevelt's home throughout his dynamic public career. PRECEDING PAGE: *Here on the spacious Piazza, in 1904, Roosevelt learned that he was the Republican nominee for president.*

ABOVE: *The dignified 22-room brick and frame house is situated on a wooded hilltop overlooking two of Long Island's harbors. One of America's best-known Victorian homes, it was the summer White House during the Roosevelt administration.*

20

Under its vaulted ceiling, the North Room houses trophies, art objects and books that reflect their late owner's wide-ranging interests and achievements. The large rug was a gift from the sultan of Turkey.

RIGHT: *The Drawing Room was Mrs. Roosevelt's haven. The Aubusson rug, Sèvres porcelains and well-upholstered furnishings project a mood of self-assured gentility. Philip A. de Laszlo painted Mrs. Roosevelt's portrait.*
BELOW RIGHT: *The Victorian Kitchen still retains the air of solid efficiency required to provide food for a large household with many guests.*

The Dining Room was used for family meals as well as more formal occasions. Warm-toned woods, gleaming silver and Minton plates from a family service add to the room's convivial mood. The Roosevelts purchased the walnut dining set during their honeymoon in Italy.

23

A boy's Bedroom, full of accumulated treasures, includes a tinted family photograph and a "newfangled" Gramophone. A basketful of sporting gear attests to the Roosevelt family's preoccupation with athletic pursuits. The colorful Navaho rugs and blankets date from the 1880s.

LEFT: *The Master Bedroom is distinguished by a monumental Gothic-style maple bedstead, a Roosevelt family heirloom. There is a cozy corner for reading near a sheer-curtained window.*
BELOW LEFT: *Mrs. Roosevelt's silver toilet articles rest on a delicately carved Victorian vanity table.*

LEFT: *Travel paraphernalia in the Trunk Room give silent evidence of many journeys.* BELOW: *In the Nursery, a tea party is hosted by Teddy Bears, proudly upholding the hospitable tradition of their famous namesake. The wheeled high chair can also function as a stroller.* OPPOSITE: *"I want a big piazza where we can sit in rocking chairs and watch the sunset"* *—Theodore Roosevelt's beautifully realized dream has become our legacy.*

RESTORING
A SOUTHERN MANSION

Twenty-five years ago, when James Arthur Williams arrived in the historic seaport of Savannah, Georgia, he expected to stay for only a short time. But much in life that is unexpected is perhaps fated. Mr. Williams is still in Savannah. An antiques dealer and interior designer with a passion for restoration, he soon discovered that the city more than generously satisfied his interests. Now he has found the ideal setting for himself—the historic *Mercer House.*

Before acquiring it, Mr. Williams, over the course of the years, had bought and restored almost fifty houses in Savannah. "In those days people like me, with a love for taking old houses and putting them back into shape, were considered a little eccentric. That's all changed now." Mercer House, the culmination of his interest in restoration, stands on Monterey Square, one of the city's twenty green plazas, four of which were laid out in 1733 by General James Edward Oglethorpe, the founder of Savannah. The focal point of Monterey Square is a statue of the gallant Polish officer Count Casimir Pulaski, who fell in the siege of Savannah during the Revolution. Early- and late-nineteenth-century townhouses line the square, and among them is the two-story Victorian Mercer House, now owned by Mr. Williams. None of his previous houses has pleased him as much.

The mansion was originally built for Hugh Weedon Mercer of Savannah, a graduate of West Point who resigned his commission in the Army of the United States to become a brigadier general in the Confederate Army. Designed in 1861 by a New York architect, John S. Norris, the residence was under construction during the Civil War. It was pillaged time and again, particularly in the course of General Sherman's march through Georgia. Sherman maintained his Savannah headquarters in another house by John Norris, and his officers and men commandeered many more houses in the town as well. According to newspaper accounts of 1866, Mercer House was gutted of its planks, sashes, window frames, and, "in fact, wood of every conceivable kind was carried off for the purpose of erecting temporary shanties." Only after the Civil War was the construction of Mercer House completed. Even so, the years that followed were not kind. "When I bought the house," says Mr. Williams, "it was an absolute shambles. Vandals had taken almost everything that could possibly be detached and moved."

Despite years of abuse, the basic attractions were there, and the lovely focal points had not been destroyed. The original English tile in the entrance hall was intact, and the semicircular stairway with its petal-shaped skylight still remained. So, too—miraculously—did the side porches and iron balconies, architectural details John Norris brought to Savannah. Restoration of the house took nearly two years of intensive work. Seven small bedrooms were opened up into two spacious ones, and another large room upstairs was fitted with a pipe organ, which Mr. Williams plays with skill. In fine weather the scent of wisteria circling the columns on the porch sweetens the air. Beyond the private garden, laid out by the present owner, is the carriage house he has converted into an antiques shop.

In Mercer House Mr. Williams has created the setting for a gracious life in a gracious city. "Savannah," he says, "is one of the most cosmopolitan and best-situated cities in the United States. If you are real and honest with your surroundings, you are quickly accepted here." Certainly the charm of the city and its way of life have found expression in his careful and loving restoration of Mercer House. He has transformed a house once ravaged by war and neglect into a place of harmony, grace and quiet living.

Thackeray described Savannah in the Victorian era as a "tranquil old city, wide streeted, tree shaded." PRECEDING PAGE: *The Mercer House, restored by owner James Williams, is distinguished by a double-columned portico and Savannah ironwork balconies.*

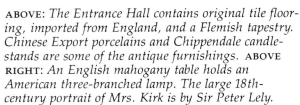

ABOVE: *The Entrance Hall contains original tile flooring, imported from England, and a Flemish tapestry. Chinese Export porcelains and Chippendale candlestands are some of the antique furnishings.* ABOVE RIGHT: *An English mahogany table holds an American three-branched lamp. The large 18th-century portrait of Mrs. Kirk is by Sir Peter Lely.*

BELOW: *Interior details of the residence destroyed during the Civil War were replaced during the two-year restoration. The west end of the Drawing Room epitomizes the fine proportions of the interior. Chinese Foo figures, circa 1690, occupy arched niches.*

LEFT AND BELOW: *An ornate gold-leaf Chippendale-framed portrait of Lady Baring by Thomas Hudson reigns over the Drawing Room. The chandelier is Bristol glass, circa 1800. In one corner, the graceful flourishes of a Chippendale chairback repeat the curved frame of the Theus portrait above it.*

LEFT: *Festive occasions are as frequent now as in the past in the elegantly appointed Dining Room. The table setting is of antique Baccarat crystal and English silver that includes pieces once owned by Edward VII and Queen Alexandra. Above the sideboard hangs a portrait by Reynolds.*

The Study is the essence of classic gentility. The carved mantel was salvaged from another historic Savannah home. Above it is a portrait by Gainsborough Dupont, nephew and pupil of Thomas Gainsborough. An 18th-century French bureau plat and Bristol chandelier are among the carefully chosen antique furnishings.

BELOW: *In the Hallway, a stair rail-
ing with Cuban mahogany balusters
sweeps upward in a graceful curve
toward the domed and enameled-glass
skylight. At the bottom, a classical
bronze by Tasy catches the light.*

ABOVE: *The sunlit Master Bedroom is furnished with
American antiques, including a carved mahogany bedstead dated 1820 and a Hepplewhite open-arm chair that
was made in Charleston in 1780. The chest is English
Chippendale. A note of 18th-century chinoiserie is intro-
duced in the portrait group above the mantel.*

WINSTON CHURCHILL'S CHARTWELL

Near London, yet in completely secluded country-side, *Chartwell* was the home of the late Sir Winston Churchill for forty years. He had bought it in a matter of three days, after he had seen it from a motor car. In years to come he was fond of saying, as he looked from the house across to the Weald of Kent, "I bought Chartwell for that view."

Churchill was rarely at Chartwell during World War II, and the house was closed. In 1945 he decided to sell the property. However, the house was soon reopened after a group of close friends decided that Chartwell, which had played such a prominent part in Britain's history, should be preserved for the nation. They purchased the residence and gave it to the National Trust with the understanding that Churchill could live there for life. The house came to play as vital a part in Churchill's later years as it had during the 1920s and 1930s. He left Chartwell for the last time in the autumn of 1964 and, after his death the following year, preparations were made to open the statesman's beloved home to the public.

The original structure of Chartwell is very old, and the Chart Well is believed to feature in the Domesday Book. When Sir Winston bought the house, it had been empty for ten years and was in poor condition. The site of the building had once been occupied by a farmhouse, which was enlarged to become a mansion in the latter part of the nineteenth century. In 1922 the house was dark, gloomy and full of dry rot, curtained in masses of ivy, and the approach planted with solemn conifers, laurel and rhododendrons. However, Churchill saw the potential of the locale, set on a steep hillside with varying levels of ground, and at once set about re-building. He employed the architect Philip Tilden, and during the transformation the ivy and many of the Victorian trappings disappeared from the façade.

Possibly the most memorable room in the house is the study, the room which—except during the war —Churchill used constantly for forty years. Here he did much of his work, his writing and his thinking. The ceiling exposes the original beams and rafters, and the room is full of treasures and mementos and books. There are relics ranging from a piece of shrapnel to a bronze cast of Jenny Jerome of New York (Churchill's mother) to a teddy bear sent by a well-wisher and propped between leather-bound volumes. When the new wing was built, five new doors linked the house to the outside—all part of the plan to create a garden that was an extension of the interior, for the Churchills were passionate gardeners. One of Sir Winston's many paintings done at Chartwell is of a single magnolia, plucked from the enormous tree that grows alongside the red brick wall at the back of the house. Churchill could reach out of his window and pick the flowers.

At the rear of the residence there is a long terraced lawn, with woods rising to the horizon beyond. To one side is a walled rose garden and beyond that a vine-covered loggia ending in a pavilion which was built during the 1920s. There are yew and beech hedges in the lovely garden, and farther away from the house is Orchard Cottage, built as a possible wartime retreat and also as Churchill's studio.

It is easy to understand Churchill's great affection for Chartwell, with its huge yew and chestnut trees, its tranquil spaciousness, its lakes and velvety lawns, and, beyond, the view that embodies the best of the English countryside. Over all is a great feeling of abiding peace; surely Sir Winston was quite serious when he said, "A day away from Chartwell is a day wasted." With the house preserved today almost exactly as it was during his lifetime, one can still see the incomparable beauty that inspired that remark.

PRECEDING PAGE: *Chartwell was Winston Churchill's home and place of work for more than 40 years. The stately red brick structure, portions of which date back to the 11th century, was acquired by Churchill in 1922. The statesman was captivated by its natural setting.*

OPPOSITE TOP: *The Drawing Room is furnished with 18th- and 19th-century pieces, including pedimented Georgian mirrors. A table is set for a game of bezique, a Churchill favorite.* OPPOSITE BOTTOM: *In the Dining Room, arched windows look out to the green vista beyond.*

BELOW: *Winston Churchill pursued his hobby of painting with great diligence, and the Studio is filled with his works of art.* BOTTOM: *Lady Churchill's Bedroom has an air of dignified simplicity. Urn-shaped Empire tables flank the bed, which is canopied in vivid silk moiré.*

The stately rose-covered Marlborough Pavilion was commissioned by Sir Winston in the 1920s in honor of his renowned ancestor, the first duke of Marlborough. LEFT: *The Golden Rose Garden was presented to the Churchills by their children on the occasion of their golden wedding anniversary.* BELOW LEFT: *Sir Winston often fed the fish in this serene setting.*

IL VITTORIALE

There is a studied solemnity about the approach to *Il Vittoriale.* The soaring black cypresses, the flagpoles, the niches peopled by statues and, at the end of the road, the monumental form of the complex that comprises the museum, the archives and D'Annunzio's private apartments—all are calculated to make the visitor feel soberly reverential.

The fame and the exotic reputation of Gabriele D'Annunzio (1863-1938) are based equally on his careers as a writer and as a soldier. His literary work included poetry, novels, plays and political pamphlets. He also served in the Italian army, navy and air force; he was a firm advocate of Italian participation in World War I; and in 1919, during a controversy between Italy and Yugoslavia on the status of the port of Fiume, he took it upon himself to lead a force of soldiers to occupy the city.

D'Annunzio created his villa primarily as a memorial to the soldiers who won victories for Italy in World War I. He also conceived of it as a monument to himself and his closest comrades-in-arms, who lie beside him in the huge mausoleum standing on the hill behind the architectural complex.

The hillside that rises high above Lake Garda is planted with hundreds of olive trees, and when D'Annunzio purchased it in 1921 it contained several modest houses. With the fervor that marked his approach to every project, he set himself the task of enlarging and transforming these houses into their present form. "Everything here bears the imprint of my style," he wrote, "in the sense that I wish to give to style. My love for Italy, my cult of memories, my aspiration to heroism, my vision for my country's future are manifested here in the smallest things, even in the harmony or clash of colors. Is it not here that the relics of war bleed again? And is it not here that the ruins of glorious cities speak or sing?"

"D'Annunzianism" was born at Il Vittoriale. Here is the compendium of a life, a genial craziness, a demoniacal cult of beauty, that was really an obsessive love of "things." Here D'Annunzio gave free rein to the eccentric taste that made him a myth, a figure adored by half of Italy. He was celebrated for his tempestuous love affairs, and it was Eleonora Duse, his greatest love, who said of him, "His life is like a tavern. Everyone passes through it."

The rooms of the Priory, as he christened his private apartments, were called cells. At times, in the "Cell of Pure Dreams," he wore a monk's habit, and there he placed a bed that was half cradle, half coffin, covered with a pall of black suede. Above it hangs a painting of the poet, nude, beside Saint Francis of Assisi. Surely, in the Priory the private world of the man D'Annunzio is revealed. The mixture of furnishings and ornaments cluttering these rooms reflects a part of the history of our time.

Perhaps the most interesting room in the Priory is the studio, where D'Annunzio sometimes worked fourteen hours a day. Only here does daylight enter, and that indirectly, from the adjoining terrace overlooking the lake. The door leading into it is so low that one must bow one's head, as though in homage to the poet's spirit. In this room walls, woodwork and furnishings are all light-toned, and the décor consists chiefly of white plaster casts of Greek sculpture and bas-relief. A plaster cast of Duse's head, which he kept veiled, once stood on his desk. He called it the "veiled witness." An especially touching sight is the array of writing equipment—all the humble tools of the writer's trade—ranging over his work table and, the most moving item, a pair of his spectacles. In the exotic setting of Il Vittoriale, the honest simplicity of these everyday instruments is as refreshing as a cool breeze on a hot day.

On a hillside overlooking Italy's Lake Garda stands Il Vittoriale, an imposing villa created by the eccentric poet-soldier Gabriele D'Annunzio. Comprised of a museum, archives and the hero's private apartment, the complex was conceived primarily as a monument to Italian patriots of World War I. PRECEDING PAGE: A Dalmatian flagpole stands in the piazza adjoining the museum (it flies D'Annunzio's personal flag). RIGHT: The Music Room is a sensual haven where the writer would immerse himself in music while reclining on silken cushions. A rich brocade overhead and Persian rugs on the floor establish a luxurious context for a lacquer chinoiserie secretary and armchair, marble columns topped by classical heads, and masks of Beethoven and Liszt.

RIGHT: *A marble mantel in the Music Room resembles an altar, with a serene Buddha flanked by Chinese monsters as its focal point. Columns and pedestals clustered nearby bear an assortment of exotic bibelots.* OPPOSITE: *A vaulted ceiling and ornate walls, brightly lacquered and gilded; windows of alabasterlike glass; and a sumptuous Persian rug made dining at Il Vittoriale a colorful occasion. D'Annunzio's fondness for animals is expressed in the tabletop adornments, which include a bronze replica of Cheli, a giant tortoise that inhabited the garden.* FOLLOWING PAGES: *The Study, the only room in the private quarters illuminated by daylight, is also relatively light toned. Plaster casts of Hellenistic sculptures and Parthenon bas-reliefs intermingle with the poet's extensive library.*

ABOVE: *The scene of many an amorous tryst, the Bedroom is a potpourri of textures and colors. From terra-cotta elephants to antique ceramic plates — every object was, in the poet's words, "a form of my spirit, an aspect of my soul, a proof of my fervor."*

OPPOSITE ABOVE: *Il Vittoriale contains an astonishing mixture of forms, historical backgrounds and aesthetic traditions. Only a highly creative mind could have arranged, or lived with, an assortment such as this one, which graces the poet's desk.*

ABOVE: *The Bath provided an opportunity to create
yet another baroque assemblage reminiscent of
Egypt, Persia—or even a Hollywood set. Animals
and women, among the poet's strongest passions,
are well represented among the imaginative clutter.*

51

NEWPORT RESTORATIONS

For anyone with a feeling for history and an eye for beauty, Newport, Rhode Island, is a rewarding microcosm of three centuries of American architecture and craftsmanship, and a rare reminder of the tough but touching quality of early New England domestic life. Most of the pastiche palaces, fake châteaux and hyperbolic "cottages" of a later era seem, to an average purist today, as they seemed to any average Newporter when they were built—little more than an unsolicited series of irrelevancies.

Doris Duke, who has known Newport ever since she can remember and who still spends much of her time there every year, is not only one of the privileged few to whom the social life of the resort is an inherited open book, but is, in addition, a sensitive and intelligent human being. In 1968 she founded the Newport Restoration Foundation, a nonprofit organization dedicated principally to the rehabilitation of Newport's remaining Colonial, Federal and Greek Revival houses, great and small. In a number of telling ways the foundation is unlike anything else of its kind. It not only restores houses — sometimes from apparently desperate states of decay—but often actually moves them bodily from their original distant or dingy sites to more congenial and central locations. When a restoration is completed, the established practice of the foundation is not to sell the house, but to rent it on reasonable terms, in order to prevent any possibility of its eventual mutilation or destruction.

The total number of local artisans employed by the foundation at any given time varies according to the work currently in progress. However, the permanent staff includes foremen, builders, masons, carpenters, carvers and painters, in addition to the architect and historian Francis Comstock, administrative officers, draftsmen and researchers—all comfortably and conveniently installed at the organization's headquarters in the former Newport YMCA, built by the late Alfred Gwynne Vanderbilt. There is a small paid staff of workers, too, at the foundation's magnificent museum of eighteenth-century Newport furniture, silver and interior decoration in the restored Samuel Whitehorne house of 1811. And there is even a resident miller—a "jolly miller," if ever there was one—who regularly grinds corn and sells meal at the 1812 windmill, which the foundation acquired and moved from its original site at Warren, Rhode Island. Here, too, are British General Prescott's guardhouse, now a miniature museum of Pilgrim furniture, and a small eighteenth-century country store displaying early American rustic implements. Nearby are a duck pond and an herb garden. The whole forms one of the foundation's most beguiling reconstructions.

But all hired helpers notwithstanding, there is truth as well as irony in Doris Duke's reply when asked to define her actual, as opposed to her honorific, place in the foundation's hierarchy: "Chief cook and bottlewasher." Whenever a house is being restored, it is she who chooses the trees and shrubs for its classically small and neat fenced yard or garden. She also selects the colors used for the exterior and interior painting of the restored houses from the traditional color range used on Newport houses a couple of centuries ago—colors so admired by the French officers billeted at Newport in the immediate post-Revolutionary years, after they had helped drive out the British forces. And from massive trees that have been felled by storms on her New Jersey estate, Miss Duke personally provides the stout oak timbers needed to replace the immense beams of the older houses. As she says, "If you want to learn about something, there is nothing like *doing* it."

Newport's Colonial buildings, now being restored by the
Newport Restoration Foundation, recall the architectural
history of the Rhode Island seaport. PRECEDING PAGE:
The circa 1770 William and Joseph Wanton House, typical
of its era, combines small scale with great dignity.

ABOVE: Balanced proportions distinguish the Daniel
Vaughn House, built around 1800 on land confiscated
from a Loyalist. OPPOSITE: The Windmill, built in 1812,
is thought to be the only one still functioning in the
United States. Its original site was Warren, Rhode Island.

FOLLOWING PAGES: *The 1738 Sisson-Collins House is one of the most graceful of the restored residences. The building was updated in the 1820s in Greek Revival mode, as its urn finials attest. Today the house appears exactly as it once did in all its original freshly painted elegance.*

TOP: *The austere exterior of the Johnson-Braman House, circa 1700, belies the comfort of its interior.*
ABOVE: *A capacious fireplace in the Living Room is typical of the time. Furnishings include a Rhode Island wing chair that dates from 1760.*

ABOVE: *The authentic 18th-century spirit of the house is painstakingly preserved in living room furnishings, including a Chippendale mahogany lowboy of Philadelphia manufacture and a gilt-ornamented mahogany mirror dated 1760.*

TOP: *In the Dining Room, a Chinese Export platter graces the rich, dark wood of the paneled mantelpiece. The Sheraton dining table is circa 1800.* ABOVE: *The fire's glow heightens the mellow tones of pine paneling and oak beams in a Bedroom*

RIGHT: *The dignified Captain Samuel Whitehorne House, built in 1811, is now a museum, an outstanding example of successful renovation.* FAR RIGHT: *A Sheraton gilt overmantel mirror and Parisian gilt-bronze clock with a figure of George Washington are displayed in the Parlor.* BELOW RIGHT: *A Newport-made mahogany table, circa 1795, and carved chairs grace the chinoiserie-papered Dining Room.*

A genteel Joseph Badger portrait, circa 1756, hangs above a Chippendale sofa in the Parlor. A pair of mahogany claw-and-ball-foot chairs are Newport heirlooms, as are many of the museum's furnishings.

THE
MARIE ANTOINETTE
BEDROOM

Her faults and failings as a queen were notorious. For many of her subjects she ultimately became not only the most hated symbol of an inept, outmoded regime — swollen with privilege and bogged down in extravagance — but a traitor to France. True, she had superlatively regal manners: With a single flowing gesture of her head and hands she knew perfectly how to render the appropriate combination of graded *révérences* to any company, however mixed. And when the time came, she was to prove that she had more than regal courage. But in the days of her prosperity she had few disinterested admirers; she was frivolous, capricious and obstinately unwise in her choice of friends. Of all the spirits that haunt the château and park of Versailles, none — not even that of the omnipresent Louis XIV himself—appeals so insistently to the imagination as the ghost of Louis XVI's queen, Marie Antoinette.

The summer of 1975 saw the completion and official presentation of a considerable portion of the restoration of several historic rooms and apartments in the château — work that has been carried on for years under the aegis of the French government by successive curators. Most recent of these is Gérald Van der Kemp, Curator-in-Chief of the Museum of Versailles, the Petit Trianon and the Grand Trianon since 1953. Of all the rooms restored, it is the *chambre de la Reine,* The Queen's Room, that is the most poignant and evocative. For this was the principal room occupied by Marie Antoinette, from soon after her arrival at Versailles in 1770 from her native Austria as an innocent fifteen-year-old dauphine, until the fateful October 6, 1789, when she fled Versailles as a thirty-four-year-old queen, never to return.

Before she came to occupy it, the Queen's Room, a spacious state bedroom near the southwest corner of the château, had been used successively by Marie Thérèse, wife of Louis XIV; two dauphines, Louis XIV's daughter-in-law and granddaughter-in-law; and Marie Leczinska, wife of Louis XV. After she became queen in 1774, Marie Antoinette indulged her personal decorative taste to the utmost—first, in the relative intimacy of the smaller rooms, but eventually in the Queen's Room itself. One of her earliest changes was to order from the Gobelins' Manufactory three tapestry portraits: of her mother, the Empress Maria Theresa; of her brother, the Emperor Joseph II; and of her husband, Louis XVI. But her subsequent changes went beyond mere familial piety. In 1782 she had a new parquet floor made for the entire bedroom; new frames were carved and gilded for the alcove in 1784; and 1786 saw a marble and bronze chimneypiece installed. And through the years she heaped elaboration upon elaboration.

To bring back the queenly splendors, the present work of restoration has been essentially a cooperation. Much of the success, of course, has depended on M. Van der Kemp. He gratefully acknowledges the work of his predecessors, while paying tribute to a heterogeneous company of twentieth-century devotees. There is the Silk Federation of Lyons, who not only wove but also presented the silks of the alcove; the small but brilliant team of expert embroiderers, *tapissiers,* carvers, cabinetmakers who, working from original documents, performed miracles of beauty and finesse. And there are, of course, the individual contributors of many nations, who have replaced carpets and chandeliers, bedcoverings and priceless silks and carving. Among the donors are the late Mrs. Barbara Hutton, Mr. Rush Kress, Mr. and Mrs. Graham Mattison, the Mitsukoshi firm of Japan, the late Pierre Weill. They all shared Gérald Van der Kemp's conviction that Versailles belongs not just to France, but to the rest of the world as well.

PRECEDING PAGE: *Marie Antoinette's Bedchamber epitomizes the grand style of Versailles's last splendid era, encompassing the period's best examples of French decorative art. The room as it appears today is the result of 20 years' careful restoration.*

LEFT: *A Gobelin tapestry portrait of the queen's mother, Empress Maria Theresa, gazes down on a Lecomte bust of the queen. Gilded motifs embellish the wall.* OPPOSITE: *The Alcove, with its elegantly canopied bed, illustrates the 18th-century penchant for lively pattern within a symmetrical framework. The Silk Federation of Lyons reproduced lost wall and bed furnishings from existing samples. The bedcover is one of the few surviving original pieces.*

WOODROW WILSON'S
FORMER HOME

As Woodrow Wilson's second term in the White House was drawing to a close in 1920, he and Mrs. Wilson began looking for a place to retire. After some discussion, they settled on Washington, D.C., as the city most congenial to both of them. The president, who had suffered a stroke in 1919 from which he never fully recovered, found pleasure and relaxation in hunting through architectural magazines for details—arches, doorways, windows—that might be incorporated in their future home. They thought about building and engaged an architect, but then discarded the plan as too costly. Finally, after experiencing a discouraging round of househunting, Mrs. Wilson found, as she described it, "an unpretentious, comfortable, dignified house, fitted to the needs of a gentleman's home." This was the house at 2340 S Street, a red brick Georgian-style townhouse, designed by the architect Waddy B. Wood.

She told Mr. Wilson that she liked the house, whereupon—without her knowledge—he took over the negotiations. A few days later they went together to see it. In her *Memoir,* Mrs. Wilson described what followed: "When we reached the door Woodrow's man brought a small piece of sod, which, with the key to one of the doors, my husband presented to me—the sod representing the land, and the key the house. Woodrow said it was an old Scotch custom." On March 4, 1921, after accompanying President-Elect and Mrs. Harding to the Capitol for the inauguration, the Wilsons drove to their new home. On arriving, they found S Street packed with people to welcome them. And the house, which forty-eight hours earlier had been in utter confusion, was in perfect order—curtains and pictures hung, rugs down and flowers everywhere. Family and friends had worked around the clock to have everything look as if it had been there for years.

Life in the S Street house soon settled into a routine adjusted to the confined movements of a semi-invalid. Mr. Wilson and his wife took breakfast in his bedroom or in the solarium between the dining room and library, which has a view of the Washington Monument. After breakfast the former president went down to the first floor, in the elevator installed for his convenience, to the "dugout," the office of his brother-in-law John Randolph Bolling, who acted as his personal secretary. Together they would go over the mail, and Mr. Wilson would dictate replies. After lunch and a rest he kept appointments in his armchair by the library fire until about half past three and then took his daily drive. Returning home, he changed to dressing gown and slippers and usually dined at a small table in the library by the fire.

This routine continued until his death on February 3, 1924. Over the years there was an almost steady stream of visitors, from his wartime colleagues Lloyd George and Clemenceau to Cabinet officers and other friends in and out of government. Edith Bolling Galt Wilson, the president's widow, continued to live on S Street until her death thirty-seven years later. The house abounds in memorabilia, since Mrs. Wilson saved everything that was in any way related to her husband: calling cards, campaign buttons, jewelry, walking sticks, articles of clothing. She sincerely meant the house to be a memorial to Woodrow Wilson, and she bequeathed it to the National Trust for Historic Preservation for this purpose. The trust administers it as a house museum, the only presidential home so maintained in the nation's capital. Restoration of the home to its 1921-1924 appearance is gradual; it is being done in stages, as information comes to light on furnishings and other elements. Meanwhile, it is a house filled with vivid memories—a place that continues to live and breathe.

ABOVE: *A Library cabinet holds Wilson mementos; one is the Bible used at his inaugurations.* OPPOSITE: *The president's portrait by Stanislav Rembski was commissioned by Mrs. Wilson. Wilson's Cabinet chair and another from the House of Representatives flank the library fireplace.*

The west wall of the Drawing Room is graced by a Gobelin tapestry representing the wedding of Psyche and Eros. The colorful hanging was presented to Mrs. Wilson by the French government in 1918. Nearby is an autographed photo of England's King Edward VII and Queen Alexandra. The ornate sofa belonged to Mrs. Wilson before her marriage to the president.

OPPOSITE: *The Dining Room's dignified table setting, cleared for dessert, includes silver candlesticks with fringed filigree shades. A large mirror reflects a 1920 portrait of Mrs. Wilson. The open door leads to the solarium, Mr. Wilson's favorite breakfast place.*
RIGHT: *The Kitchen holds an array of utensils and household products recalling the era. The large kitchen range combines both gas and wood-burning capacities.*

LEFT: *President Wilson enjoyed playing music from a large record collection on his Victrola.* BELOW LEFT: *Gracefully draped windows and a Victorian rosewood settee in the Drawing Room typify the charm of the house.* BELOW: *The ''Dugout'' was the name given to the Office used by Mr. Wilson's brother-in-law and private secretary, John Randolph Bolling. The decorative screen is made of an assemblage of playing cards.* OPPOSITE TOP: *Mr. Wilson used the Hammond typewriter both in the White House and on his travels.* OPPOSITE BOTTOM: *The Bedroom has been preserved as it was at the time of the president's death. The bed duplicates the measurements of the Lincoln bed in the White House; the desk was Wilson's at Princeton. Mrs. Wilson's portrait is a copy of the 1916 painting by A. Muller-Ury that hangs in the White House.*

MEMORIES
OF THE
MARQUIS DE SADE

In the twelfth-century vestibule of the *Château de Condé-en-Brie* is a genealogical tree, dating from 1100, of the de Sade family. It is interesting to notice that in 1814 the title *marquis* was replaced by *comte*, which had been awarded to the family in 1720. The son of *the* Marquis de Sade did not want to inherit his notorious father's title. But today's Marquis de Sade, while known as the Comte, feels quite differently. "I have two goals in life," he explains, "to restore this château and to restore de Sade to his proper place in the history of French letters."

The first task, while formidable, may prove the easier one. When World War II ended, Xavier de Sade and his bride returned to the tiny village of Condé-en-Brie. Located near the vineyards of Champagne, but even nearer the battlefields, the Château de Condé was occupied, bombarded and pillaged during both world wars. "We found bayonet slashes here," says the Comte de Sade, pointing to the trompe l'oeil canvas wallcoverings lining the music salon. Ornate ceiling paintings were practically obliterated, and the immense fireplace had crumbled into a ruin. Of considerable aid to the owner in his task of reconstruction were ten large trunks filled with archives both of the château and of the village itself. Now, thirty years later, the count is hoping to pass this history along. "I'm trying to educate people here to respect the development of the château," he says. "The town of Condé gave its name to the illustrious family that is a collateral branch of the royal house of Bourbon. But the earliest construction of the château began around 1200. The walls and the loopholes date from the period when you had to defend yourself."

Passing from one owner to another through the centuries, by either direct inheritance or marriage, the château was completely run down when it was bought in 1719 by Jean-François Leriget de la Faye, who had been an intimate of Louis XIV. "When he bought Condé, this man of remarkable taste was very rich," says the present Comte de Sade. "He transformed it into a fashionable eighteenth-century country house." In 1814 the château passed to the de Sade family when it was inherited through marriage by the son of the notorious marquis. Although the marquis himself never lived here, the halls are lined with his documents. When the present owner returned to the château, he spent a good deal of time looking around the attic. There, he discovered a large, mysterious case. "It had been there since the beginning of the nineteenth century," recalls the count, "and it had *never* been opened—largely because of my great-great-grandfather, the younger son of the marquis. When his father died in the insane asylum of Charenton, he went there and burned everything he could. What remained, he put in this case—including letters, which he also could have destroyed."

Among the papers were plays, a diary and a travel log. All will eventually be published. "I want to bring the Marquis de Sade out of the shadows," says the count. "Above all, he was a great writer. At first the family was shocked. Now most of them approve, and some are proud to have him as an ancestor." The unpublished letters, in the Marquis de Sade's minuscule handwriting, are the main curiosity of the château—parts of which are open to the public several months each year. Indeed, the building, furniture and tapestries are designated historical monuments. By opening the château to the public, the owner is eligible for limited government aid. "But mostly we have done it with our own hands," he says.

His wife and five children help, and they all take turns conducting the public visits. "Our family life has disappeared," sighs the Comte de Sade. "This is the work of an entire lifetime."

PRECEDING PAGE: *Two life objectives impel Comte Xavier de Sade: to vindicate the honor and literary reputation of his famed ancestor, the Marquis de Sade, and to restore to full beauty the 12th-century Château de Condé-en-Brie, which was inherited by the de Sade family in 1814.*

ABOVE AND FOLLOWING PAGES: *In the Grand Salon, four large murals by the 18th-century artist Jean-Baptiste Oudry re-create the vivid spectacle of the hunt. Equally pictorial, though on a smaller, quieter scale, is the suite of Régence furniture upholstered in Beauvais tapestries illustrating the* Fables of La Fontaine. *The harpsichord, which dates from 1624, was built by Ruckers; an exceptional feature is a serene eveningscape, painted on the underside of the instrument's lid by Nicolas Poussin.*

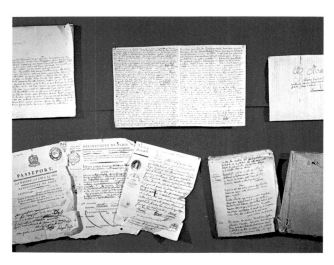

WASHINGTON IRVING'S HOUSE

"About five-and-twenty miles from the ancient and renowned city of Manhattan, formerly called New Amsterdam . . . on the eastern bank of the Hudson known among Dutch mariners of yore as the Tappan Zee . . . stands a little, old-fashioned stone mansion, all made up of gabled ends, and as full of angles and corners as an old cocked hat." For the purposes of the story he was about to unfold, Washington Irving called this place "Wolfert's Roost," but as anyone who has visited Irving's home in Tarrytown, New York, will immediately recognize, the little old-fashioned stone mansion is none other than the author's own beloved *Sunnyside.*

Full of the spirit, the romantic imagination and the joie de vivre of one of America's most beloved legend makers, it still preserves its original charm — thanks to Sleepy Hollow Restorations, a foundation established by John D. Rockefeller, Jr., that maintains the house. Irving began building Sunnyside in 1835, when he was a fifty-two-year-old bachelor and at the height of his fame. The creator of such beguiling characters as Rip Van Winkle and Ichabod Crane, he had come home after nearly twenty years abroad. Sunnyside was to be the fulfillment of many dreams, a permanent home "fitted up to my own humor" in the very Hudson River countryside he had celebrated in his writings. The property, which with later additions would run to twenty-four acres, had been part of the vast Philipse family manor during the Dutch regime. Later the portion Irving fancied belonged to friends, and in his boyhood he roamed its expanses, played in its stream-creased dells and admired its prospects of the river.

Worldly, sophisticated and steeped in English Romanticism from years of living among writers like Sir Walter Scott and William Beckford, Irving probably could not have located any American architect capable of executing the house of his imagination. Thus he designed it himself, in collaboration with his painter friend, George Harvey. Like every other homeowner who has ever undertaken a major structural revamping, he complained that the project was costing more money than he had anticipated. "For such a small edifice it has a prodigious swallow, and reminds me more of those little fairy changelings called Killcrops, which eat and eat, and are never the fatter." It also took longer than expected. Not until October 1836, a year after work had begun, was Irving able to move in. It is probable that the major share of the Federal and Empire furniture and other appointments were purchased specifically for Sunnyside since Irving had lived his first five decades relatively unencumbered with possessions. Over the years that followed he made a number of improvements on his "dear little cottage" and outbuildings. He loved to work at landscaping and he had, as he cheerfully admitted, "a relish for castle building." In 1847, with the main house positively bulging with relatives, he added a three-story "pagoda" tower to provide extra sleeping quarters.

Of all the rooms in the main house, the most personal is the writer's own study, located on the southeast corner, off the front entrance hall. Here he worked on his histories and essays, kept up a lively correspondence and entertained his closest friends. When his relatives were away, bachelor Irving all but lived in his study, napping in the sleeping alcove tucked between the bookcases at the back of the room, lolling in his cozy window seat to watch his favorite songbirds. His desk, a gift from his grateful publishers, G. P. Putnam & Sons, and his extensive library remain today precisely as he left them, mementos of a man for whom words born of imagination were the essence of joyous life.

LEFT: *The landscapes in the elegant Parlor are attributed to Irving's friend George Harvey; the 1809 portrait of Irving is by John Wesley Jarvis. Laminated wood side chairs are Belter originals.* ABOVE: *A Federal period table holds a Staffordshire tea service. Lace curtains behind damask draperies veil the view of the Hudson River.*

*Irving frequently entertained such notables as Holmes
and Thackeray in the Parlor. The rosewood piano, made
by Robert Nunn, Clark and Co. of New York, was played
by Irving's nieces at family socials. The mezzotint is of
Sir Walter Scott surrounded by literary friends.*

ABOVE: *A cast-iron wood-burning stove in the kitchen replaced the traditional open fireplace. Other modernization during Irving's lifetime included an ingenious system for hot and cold running water using gravitational flow.*

OPPOSITE TOP RIGHT: *The Irving nieces'*
cheerful Bedroom features a 19th-century
American sleigh bed with its colorful Friend-
ship quilt. OPPOSITE TOP LEFT AND OPPOSITE
BOTTOM: *The author's Bedroom is reflected in*
an ornate shaving-stand mirror. The ceiling
arches over the curves of a netted Sheraton
tester bed and American balloon-back side
chairs. RIGHT AND BELOW: *The landscaped*
grounds reflect Washington Irving's great indi-
viduality. The author christened the pond, with
its graceful swans, ''Little Mediterranean.''

CALCUTTA'S
MARBLE PALACE

Early in the Indian morning, while it is still comparatively cool, the day begins at the *Marble Palace*. Liveried servants hurry here and there, moving furniture, arranging birdcages on terraces and verandas, dusting the paintings and sculpture. Amidst the bustle, the descendants of Raja Rajendra Mullick move about in a stately fashion, perhaps planning a quiet day of religious devotion. Soon the palace is open and ready, but these days relatively few visitors will come, whether in the relative cool of winter or the steamy heat of summer.

Until 1911, when King George V announced at the Delhi Durbar that the capital was to be transferred to a new city, Calcutta was the government seat of the British Empire in India. From this trading settlement in Bengal, an unhealthy spot with a miserable climate on the Hooghly River, more than 300 million people were ruled for over a century. Here the governor-general — later the viceroy — had his residence: Government House, an imposing palace built at the beginning of the nineteenth century. Calcutta soon became known as the "City of Palaces." Early prints show a distant prospect of gleaming white Classical columns and pediments, with the great dome and porticoes of Government House dominating the skyline. The architectural standard it set was adopted in other official buildings, with the exception of the Gothic High Court. It was also maintained in the houses of rich merchants, European and Indian. Conspicuous among them is the residence of the Mullick family, the Marble Palace.

The family is one of the oldest and noblest in Calcutta, claiming descent from the Survarnabaniks of Bengal, a sort of mercantile aristocracy of the eighth century. Jayram Mullick settled in Govindapur before the establishment of Calcutta by Job Charnock in 1690. When Fort William was built on the site of this village in 1757, the Mullicks were granted land in North Calcutta. Gangavishnu Mullick had a flourishing banking business in the late eighteenth century, trading with China and Southeast Asia as well as in India itself. He was also known for his philanthropy, as was his son, Nilmony Mullick. The latter died in 1821 when his adopted son, Rajendra Mullick, was only two years old. And it was Raja Rajendra Mullick, whose culture, learning and great benevolence earned him the honorific "Bahadur," who was the creator of the Marble Palace.

The Marble Palace was built around 1835. Though the name of the architect is not recorded, he is thought to have been Indian. Indeed, the palace is like many another in India — spacious, dignified and luxurious, with high ceilings and many verandas and open loggias. The architecture is not strictly orthodox by European standards, and it has a definite Indian flavor. What is memorable about the edifice, however, is not the architecture, but the contents: an astonishing collection of original works and copies of European sculpture. These were acquired by Rajendra Mullick's agents in Europe; just as Calcutta was the source of the attempt to Westernize Indian painting, so Mullick wished to spread Western culture of all kinds in India. A profusion of bronze, marble, stone and plaster figures fills every room as well as the grounds themselves. These statues, set against a background of Classical architecture, fulfill the European Neo-Classical ideal of the museum as a repository of the highest and most perfect forms of sculpture.

The raja's descendants still live in the Marble Palace and conduct themselves with unaffected simplicity amid the fading grandeur of the past, so characteristic of India. Their home is a dignified relic of the gracious splendor that was once Calcutta.

PRECEDING PAGE: *The Marble Palace, a lasting monument to European-influenced Classical architecture, still stands in Calcutta, once the ''City of Palaces.'' The brick and stucco building was constructed in the 1830s by Raja Rajendra Mullick Bahadur, a merchant prince and aficionado of Western culture.*

TOP LEFT, TOP RIGHT AND ABOVE: *Tropical vegetation and lacy ironwork verandas contrast with European garden statuary, and dignified Doric columns line the exterior. The grounds encompass a zoo and an aviary. The descendants of the raja still occupy the palace, and maintain it for public viewing.*

Massive columns surround the central Courtyard, with its marble statuary and refreshing fountain. Ornamental stuccowork garlands the exterior. The palace displays an extensive use of polished, geometric-patterned marble floors — the only marble in the edifice, despite its name.

ABOVE: *In Colonial India, trade with the West generated an enthusiasm for European objets d'art. The palace's airy Gallery contains both original sculpture and copies of ancient works imported from Italy, in the plentiful variety typical of 19th-century taste.*
RIGHT: *A shaft of light illuminates a reproduction of a statue by Canova.*

The lavishly ornamented Hall is
well-equipped for billiards with its
table, low-hanging lights and ceiling
fans. The cue racks are guarded by a
pantheon of Hellenic attendants.

A maiden in a setting of opulent decoration and a graceful American Indian exemplify the Victorian preference for the decorously exposed feminine form and romantic subject matter.

The Veranda houses a Study, enclosed
by the tracery of a wrought-iron
façade. To those who live in the palace
today, the breeze-cooled porch recalls
another era's elegance and grandeur.

THE ELMS

On June 27, 1962, a memorable auction took place in the ballroom of *The Elms*, one of those palatial "summer cottages" that were once so characteristic of Newport, Rhode Island. There seemed little doubt that this auction was sounding the death knell of yet another old Newport estate. Almost twenty years later, however, The Elms is not only very much alive, it is also again one of Newport's showplaces — thanks to an eleventh-hour rescue undertaken by the Preservation Society of Newport County.

To save the property from demolition by its new owners, a real estate syndicate, the Preservation Society raised the money to buy it themselves — naturally without the furnishings that had been sold at auction. However, less than a month later, the society had also managed, through gifts and loans, to gather up enough furniture of the same quality to refurnish the mansion suitably. So on August 20, 1962, The Elms was opened as a public museum.

The "cottage," as Newport called its marble palaces in the Golden Age, was originally built for Edward Julius Berwind, for many decades America's leading coal industrialist. He began his entry into the exclusive resort's inner circles in 1888 by buying a large, rather ordinary Victorian house on Bellevue Avenue and waiting to see what would happen. Somewhat to his own surprise, Berwind was apparently acceptable to Newport society. Though he grew up in Philadelphia in modest circumstances, the son of an immigrant Prussian cabinetmaker, he had risen quickly in the business world and had also acquired a cultivated English wife. Satisfied that he had a brilliant future in Newport, Berwind purchased more than fourteen additional acres of land around his old cottage. And in 1899 he engaged an architect, one Horace Trumbauer. Trumbauer was also from Philadelphia, also of German parentage

and modest beginnings, also rising rapidly in the world. But everything he knew about architecture he had learned in books and in the offices of other architects; he had never even been abroad.

Undaunted, he set about creating for Berwind a properly elegant eighteenth-century French château, using the Château d'Asnières, near Paris, as a model. In the spring of 1901, the owners went off to Europe and left instructions that a great housewarming party be prepared for their return. That summer the fête took place, complete with two orchestras, a brass band, a sea of flowers inside and outside the house and a whimsical troop of monkeys frolicking over the grounds. More than two hundred guests reportedly spent a superb evening — some of the guests said it was the best of the season.

Spectacularly launched, the Berwinds settled into the spirit of Newport. For day-to-day comforts the childless couple made do with a household staff of sixteen, including three chefs, a butler, four footmen, and a lady's maid to look after Mrs. Berwind's needs. To keep the estate going, there were also a superintendent, a dozen gardeners in season, a night watchman and an engineer whose main responsibility was to keep the boilers operating year-round to preserve the furniture and paintings.

Mrs. Berwind died in 1922, and her husband's unmarried sister took over as mistress of the house. Julia Berwind seems to have enjoyed The Elms more than anyone else, and upon her brother's death in 1936 she inherited the mansion. She remained châtelaine of The Elms until 1961, when she died at the age of ninety-eight. The property passed to distant heirs, who sold it to the real estate syndicate. It is a happy circumstance for the Newport Community that the mansion was saved, and stands today as a lasting reminder of life in the grand old style.

Modeled after the 18th-century Château d'Asnières out-side Paris, The Elms was designed for coal magnate Edward J. Berwind and his wife, Herminie, as their New-port "summer cottage." PRECEDING PAGE: *In 1901 the couple's housewarming ball for over 200 guests was the triumph of the social season. The rear façade opens onto parklike grounds, where tame monkeys frolicked about to entertain dancers taking the air.* ABOVE: *The light and airy Conservatory still houses five original marble pieces that were not auctioned off with almost all the mansion's other furnishings in 1962: statues in each corner depict-ing the four seasons, and a huge urn that revolves when merely touched.* OPPOSITE: *Columns of Breccia marble and gilded bronze line the opulent marble Hall at the top of the divided Grand Staircase. Serving as a central axis for the perfectly symmetrical château, the palatial hallway affords access to all the rooms.*

OPPOSITE TOP: *The Ballroom's lavish 41-by-49-foot dimensions are well suited to the sumptuous décor. Although only the wall brackets, chandelier, Louis XV gilt bronze andirons and a marble bust of Marie Antoinette remain of the original furnishings, the gold-leaf piano and velvet and gilt chairs afford a glimpse of Newport's magnificence in its Golden Age.* OPPOSITE BOTTOM: *The chimneypiece, of cut Caen limestone and surmounted by a carved walnut overmantel, stands out in the subdued atmosphere of the Library.* BELOW: *The intricate Dining Room ceiling is over 19 feet high, as are all ceilings on the first floor.*

BELOW: *Throughout Mrs. Berwind's Bedroom a recurrent festoon motif reflects the delicate grace of the 18th-century French furnishings. Carried from the gilt swags on the white mantel to the bas-relief of the ceiling molding, the motif is captured again in the draperies over the bed. Neutral tints allow the textures and fabrics to speak for themselves.* OPPOSITE: *In Mr. Berwind's second-floor Bedroom, adjacent to his wife's, the ormolu light fixtures and a boldly carved oxblood marble mantel with ormolu mounts are part of the room's original décor.*

LEGACY
OF A
NORMAN BARON

England's *Leeds Castle* came into existence more than eleven hundred years ago, when it was first built as the stronghold of a Kentish thane. Before long it had been rebuilt, and for many generations thereafter it was inhabited by a fierce Norman family before passing into the possession of the Crown during the reign of Edward I. A tradition was formed in these early days of royal ownership by which Leeds was considered primarily a woman's castle. Succeeding sovereigns made Leeds over to their consorts, granting the castle to them as a dower, to be retained during their widowhood. Here the young widow Catherine of Valois fell in love with her clerk of the wardrobe and is believed to have secretly married him. Here Eleanor of Castile lived in happiness with her king; here Joan of Navarre was accused of witchcraft. And at least one of Henry VIII's six wives lived at the castle in brief splendor.

When Leeds passed from the Crown, it came to be owned by a series of English families until it was finally bought by its last private occupant, the Honorable Olive, Lady Baillie. She was the heiress to a substantial fortune left by her American mother, who was a Whitney, and she devoted her life to the restoration of the castle. With the designer Boudin and the château restorer Radoux, Lady Baillie set about casting her spell on what has been described as the most magically beautiful castle in the world. Eventually she left Leeds to the nation, and it is here, in an unrivaled setting of beauty, that important medical seminars and government meetings are now held.

To perpetuate the tradition of Leeds as a woman's castle where eight Medieval queens once lived, the flag of Eleanor of Castile flies from the masthead on the tower of the Gloriette in alternation with Lady Baillie's personal flag. Situated in the country between London and the south coast of England, the castle is half Medieval and half Romantic Revival. The park is entirely eighteenth century and was done by Capability Brown. The enchanted buildings, ethereal in their rustic setting, form one vision of Leeds, its towers glimpsed through a pine wood and rising from islands centered in the lake. Another equally arresting picture of castle and mere can be seen at the beginning of an English summer, after months of the harsh winter wind—with young beech leaves shiny green, the surrounding parkland carpeted in bluebells and anemones, and black swans gliding on the calm water. It is an authentically English scene of surpassing charm.

When Lady Baillie became owner of the castle, her own suite of rooms was, appropriately for the châtelaine, in the oldest part of the building. She renovated the basic structure of the Gloriette, built on one of the islands and originally connected to the rest of the structure by two drawbridges. The Gloriette, where the most important regal rooms had been in olden days, was redecorated several years ago by antiques dealer and art expert Christopher Gibbs. The bedrooms are lovely; Lady Baillie paid meticulous attention to detail in refurbishing them. Even the top edges of her linen sheets were individually designed by Boudin. The application of her energy was enormous—records minutely kept, all the birds in the aviary inventoried, the treasures of the castle catalogued with love and care.

And so the great castle of the queens of Medieval England survives. The sense of history here is all-pervading, quite as dominating as the beauty of Leeds itself and its fantasy setting. In fact, the story of England permeates every corner of the castle. The happy feeling persists that it will survive splendidly in future generations—every bit as splendidly as it has over the centuries of a very long past.

ABOVE AND OPPOSITE: *During the 18th century, landscape architect Capability Brown transformed the grounds into the park that exists today. Lord Conway described Leeds Castle over a half century ago: "Among the waters on an autumnal evening when the bracken is golden and there is a faint blue mist among the trees... the loveliest castle, as thus beheld, in the whole world."*

LEFT: *An enclosed circular staircase is crowned with a carved Gothic crusader and a lion.* BELOW LEFT: *The Library is a scholarly apartment with its classical moldings, book-lined shelves and terrestrial globes.* OPPOSITE: *The Dining Room projects an 18th-century mood. Chinese* famille rose *porcelains are displayed on brackets against a pastel wall, and a gros point floral rug covers parquet flooring. Pale Louis XV chairs surround a dignified English pedestal table.*

The Hon. Olive, Lady Baillie, was the last private occupant of Leeds Castle, and during her ownership renovations both preserved the past and created livable settings. In the Turret Bedroom are a likeness of an Elizabethan gentleman and a 17th-century portrait of a little girl.

ABOVE LEFT AND LEFT: *A parcel gilt mirror hangs above a Louis XV chinoiserie lacquer commode in Lady Baillie's Bedroom. A series of miniature still lifes dots the wall. K'ang Hsi porcelain birds are colorful reminders of the aviary Lady Baillie established on the grounds of the castle.*

THE
MORRIS-JUMEL MANSION

The Washington Headquarters Association, the volunteer group that looks after the Morris-Jumel Mansion Museum in New York City, began its involvement with this beautiful eighteenth-century residence back in 1903, when the structure was slated for demolition to make way for an apartment building. Citing the house's brief career as General George Washington's command post during the first months of the American Revolution, the association was able to persuade the city to buy the structure and turn it over to them for safekeeping.

As any furnishings of historic value had long since been auctioned off by various tenants, the Morris-Jumel Mansion remained imperfectly decorated for some seven decades, and the neighborhood, on the northern end of Manhattan Island, grew increasingly remote from the city's cultural circuit. The association's members realized that a major restoration was in order if they wanted to continue to attract visitors. So, recently, they undertook the task of bringing the mansion back to its original splendor.

As the year carved in the keystone arch in the main hall indicates, the mansion dates from 1765. Its owners were Roger Morris, a hero of the French and Indian Wars, and his wife, Mary Philipse, one of the wealthiest and most glamorous young women in the Colonies. When the Revolution broke out in 1776, the loyalties of the Morris family were personally and pragmatically with the British, and they removed to England for safety. They left their servants behind, fully expecting to return when the insurrection was over. Scarcely had they gone when General Washington, an old friend of Morris's and a one-time suitor of Mary's, appropriated the mansion as his headquarters. His days there were bitter with disappointment and anxiety. From the widow's walk on the roof, he could actually see his unseasoned troops routed by the Redcoats in skirmish after skirmish. And, late in October 1776, General Washington was forced to abandon the house. The British moved in before the hearth fires died, and there they remained for the rest of the conflict.

Miraculously, the mansion survived unscathed, and in 1804 it was sold to a prosperous French merchant, Stephen Jumel. Widowed at fifty, he had lately married his mistress, a young woman whose real-life story outshines most works of fiction. Betsy Brown, alias Eliza Bowen—alleged by some to have been Washington's illegitimate child—had in fact begun life in a Rhode Island brothel and had grown up to prosper in some of New York's best-known houses of pleasure. The new Mme. Jumel, however, was determined to be accepted by society, and to that end she spent several years redoing the Morris interiors. But fine house or no, as far as New York's respectable upper crust was concerned, Stephen Jumel's wife was still the notorious Betsy Brown. No invitations were issued to the couple.

In 1815 the Jumels finally closed the house and moved to Paris. When her husband died in 1832, Mme. Jumel decided to return to Harlem Heights. In her early fifties and still a very attractive woman, she soon married her attorney, the seventy-seven-year-old Aaron Burr. The romance cooled quickly, however, and she divorced the aging adventurer in 1836. She lived out the remaining twenty-nine years of her life in the mansion as a semirecluse.

In drawing up plans for the recent refurbishing of the Morris-Jumel Mansion, the association made a wise decision to refurbish the house as a reflection of the century of history that shaped it. To realize that backward glance at history, each room was furnished with all the fidelity possible, resulting in a splendid re-creation of the past.

PRECEDING PAGE: *The stately Georgian Morris-Jumel Mansion is the oldest residence still in existence on Manhattan Island. Built in 1765 by Loyalist Colonel Roger Morris, it was purchased in 1804 by Stephen Jumel, who updated the house in Federal style. Washington and Burr are among the many notables who have been guests in the mansion.* RIGHT: *The interior of the residence is being restored to the Georgian and Federal styles of its first 100 years. The door's delicate side and fan windows illuminate the wide Hall, distinguished by Empire period furnishings and swag-bordered grisaille wallpaper.*

OPPOSITE BELOW: *The Octagon Drawing Room once served as George Washington's military headquarters. Colorful wallpaper, handpainted in China in the 18th century, enhances the graceful motifs of English Chippendale chairs. A mahogany and gilt-wood American mirror harmonizes with a marble-topped American sideboard below.*
ABOVE: *The Dining Room's Georgian accoutrements include Duncan Phyfe chairs and a 1783 portrait of Mrs. John Chester by Joseph Steward. A portrait of Washington, who dined in this room, hangs above an 18th-century serpentine-fronted sideboard.*

RIGHT AND OPPOSITE ABOVE:
*Mme. Jumel, despite a scandalous
past, became an intimate of the
Napoleonic court and a devotee of
the Empire style. Her Bedroom is
furnished with objects from the
imperial household, including
swan's neck slipper chairs once
belonging to Empress Josephine's
daughter. An Aubusson rug
underscores the room's feminine
appeal.* OPPOSITE BELOW: *A
Bedroom used by Mary Bowen,
the Jumels' adopted daughter,
contains an elaborately carved
four-poster bed and an unusual
writing-desk-and-chair that con-
verts into an oval table.*

LEFT: *The Toy Room was once Mme. Jumel's Dressing Room. Its present miniature occupants include a doll languishing on an Empire sofa, a Chippendale-style high chair and a wooden rocking horse.* RIGHT: *Aaron Burr's Bedroom dates from his brief marriage to Mme. Jumel. French* toiles de Jouy *bedcoverings, Burr's original desk and a Federal period mahogany clock are among the furnishings. The portrait of Burr is a copy of Vanderlyn's original.*

LEDREBORG CASTLE

The origins of Danish manor houses are often lost in the obscurity of the past. Frequently these origins lie beyond any written record, and few of the older manor houses can be traced before the fifteenth century. They rose near the villages or on individual farms — at first, the half-timbered houses of a prosperous peasantry, built on small plots of land.

When the sixteenth century in Denmark brought many changes in agriculture, a struggle began between owners of the larger and the smaller farms. Great estates were amassed, and the noblemen who came to own them built imposing manor houses. Many of these were the work of foreign craftsmen, who built huge châteaux for the Danish lords, resplendent with all the artistry of the Renaissance. The aristocratic landowners hold a firm place in the history of the country. Their names were inscribed on elaborate mantelpieces, their portraits painted by Dutch artists; they enjoyed all that was best in the education and knowledge of their times.

But war, falling prices and simple bad luck plagued the last days of aristocratic power. After the establishment of absolute monarchy, the state became the master, and the squires receded into the background. A century passed, during which little new building took place, but in time the situation changed again. The nobility allied itself closely with the Danish court. Older estates were rebuilt, and new manor houses constructed in the Rococo style of the French kings. The renovations of this era were notable, particularly in the interiors of the mansions, decorated in the popular and luxurious taste of the Baroque.

A superb example of the period is *Ledreborg Castle* at Lejre, situated in a part of Denmark filled with historical monuments. The site, in fact, was once the stronghold of Gorm the Old. The property was acquired by Count Johan Ludvig Holstein-Ledreborg

at the beginning of the eighteenth century, when it was known as Lejregard. The count rebuilt the manor house in a mixture of the Baroque and the Rococo. The interiors bear the artistic stamp of Eigtved and Krieger and remain untouched to this day: the Italian stucco work, the French tapestries, the furniture of the time, and the embroidered carpets. There is also an abundant collection of paintings at Ledreborg Castle, and a record of the first count's family can be seen today in the portraits by Tuscher and Wahl in the vaulted banquet hall. Indeed, almost every wall seems to be covered, and in a corridor leading from the entrance hall, with its lovely Blåtårn tiles, the castle appears in four different paintings, showing it as it was before the renovations of the eighteenth century.

The park surrounding the castle is in the rather formal French-Italian style. Ancient trees descend to the bottom of the valley; there are carefully tended streams and symmetrical rows of beech trees. Among the beeches is Jerichau's fine statue of Adam and Eve after the Fall. As a matter of fact, there is a family story attached to this particular statue. It appears that a reigning count had ordered the sculpture to be made in Rome from a beautiful piece of white marble. When it arrived, however, a small gray stain was found in the otherwise perfect stone. The count was infuriated and decreed that the statue be banished from his house. So now Adam and Eve stand among the beech trees, at the mercy of the wind — cast out of Paradise again.

In an era when it is difficult to maintain and preserve the splendors of a castle like Ledreborg, it is indeed pleasant to stroll down the two-hundred-year-old allée of trees. For a moment it almost seems like being in some hushed and lovely ancient cathedral, amidst the lasting glory of the ages.

PRECEDING PAGE: *Ledreborg Castle in Denmark is one of that country's finest existing manor houses. The result of a restoration in the 1740s by Count Johan Ludvig Holstein-Ledreborg, the estate has parklike grounds that include a running stream and ascending terraces.*

LEFT: *The Baroque Bell Tower, designed as a carriage house by the architect L. Thura, frames the entrance to the main courtyard.* BELOW LEFT: *The Koege Tapestry Room's hangings, featuring detailed views with arresting perspectives, were designed by François Legere, a French artist who had a factory in Koege. The needlework carpet and graceful Rococo furnishings are part of the castle's original trappings.*

The walls in the Red Drawing Room are covered by a wealth of paintings, including works by van Ruisdael and Backhuyzen. Among the ceramic pieces are a famille rose tureen and Montpellier faïence. Louis XVI furnishings reflect the 18th-century preference for bright colors.

The vaulted ceiling of the Banquet Hall is distinguished
by stucco work done by itinerant Italian artisans. Portraits represent all the first Ledreborg family members but
one—the artist Tuscher died before completing the first
count's likeness. A Rococo framed mirror fills his space.

RIGHT: *In the Dining Room, family portraits of five generations of Ledreborg counts attest to the unbroken line of the castle's ownership since its 18th-century restoration.* BELOW RIGHT: *The Baroque Chapel, designed by Krieger, occupies the entire west wing. Panels depicting Biblical scenes are painted in the style of Rubens.*

LEFT: *The Miniature Room's many small-scale furnishings give the room a fairy-tale charm. The needlework rug bears the family coat-of-arms.* BELOW: *An irascible swan named Mozart has been known to chase away visitors who venture too close to his idyllic retreat.*

BILTMORE HOUSE

George Washington Vanderbilt was just twenty-three and still a bachelor when his father, William Henry, died in 1885, leaving nearly two hundred million dollars to be divided among his heirs. George, "a delicate, refined and bookish man," had shown none of the family aptitude for business, so no one was surprised when he was in effect put out to pasture with a mere five million dollars in cash and a five-million-dollar trust.

Young Vanderbilt wasted little time putting the money to use. In 1887 he traveled to Asheville, North Carolina — a handsome resort city with a climate said to cure everything from asthma to nervous prostration — and he decided to make his home there. Quietly he began buying up parcels of land until he had accumulated nearly one hundred and thirty thousand acres of southern Appalachian foothills. He then called in two giants of nineteenth-century design, architect Richard Morris Hunt and landscape designer Frederick Law Olmsted, to help him turn a fantasy into reality. The result is *Biltmore House*, the largest residential estate ever built in America.

Building got under way rapidly. A huge site was cleared to make way for the main house, designed after the manner of the French châteaux of the Loire Valley, which was to occupy more than four acres all by itself. The small town of Best, on the banks of a nearby river, was razed, and masses of earth were moved in to elevate the site a safe few extra feet above the high-water mark. Here a model Dutch-style village, renamed Biltmore, was constructed along Hunt's plans to house the staff.

The temporary work force of local artisans and craftsmen swelled to a thousand during the five years of building, and the costs eventually ran to five million dollars. Hunt's masons clambered over the four-story, 780-foot-long structure, piling huge blocks of Indiana limestone into Biltmore's curiously asymmetric, picturesque profile of pinnacles, turrets, galleries and Gothic chimneys. Within the walls others were installing whole rooms taken from European castles, or making fine reproductions of Old World interiors. In all, Biltmore House would contain two hundred and fifty rooms, every one generously conceived. Landscape architect Olmsted's crew was equally busy. Some toiled to create the thirty-eight acres of formal parterres, modeled after the fine gardens of Vaux-le-Vicomte near Paris, while others prepared for vast planting projects in the wilder parts of the extensive Vanderbilt property.

The mansion was officially opened on Christmas Eve 1895 with the arrival of half-a-dozen private railroad cars carrying various members of the Vanderbilt family and their servants. They found the accommodations impressive, yet distinctly different from the gilt-and-marble summer palaces of Newport. Biltmore House was so tasteful, so harmonious in its furnishings as to be genuinely livable.

George Washington Vanderbilt died at fifty-two, in 1914. In 1913 he had begun negotiating with the federal government to create Pisgah National Forest and had donated more than one hundred thousand acres to the National Park Service. He left twelve thousand five hundred acres around the mansion for his wife and their only child, Cornelia. Mrs. Vanderbilt remarried in 1925 and moved to Washington, D.C. Cornelia had married John Francis Amherst Cecil the year before, and since they now visited Biltmore only irregularly, the Cecils permitted the house to be opened to the public in 1930.

Today, the Cecils' two sons, William and George, maintain their patrimony beautifully, preserving the past with a personal pride that surely would have delighted their eminent grandfather.

PRECEDING PAGE: *Biltmore House was the realization of a dream for George Washington Vanderbilt, who employed architect Richard Morris Hunt and landscape designer Frederick Law Olmsted to design it. The estate was modeled after a 16th-century French château.*

LEFT: *The Library's more than 20,000 volumes are evidence of the scholarly Mr. Vanderbilt's wide range of interests; they include histories, classical literature and works on art, architecture and landscape gardening. Over the black marble mantel a relief carving by Viennese sculptor Karl Bitter depicts Hestia, guardian of the hearth, and Demeter, goddess of the earth. Surmounting the room's Baroque splendor is a painted ceiling, attributed to Giovanni Antonio Pellegrini, which was originally in an Italian palace.* OPPOSITE: *A sunken area constructed mostly of marble, the Palm Court is green year-round with plants from the gardens and greenhouses. Another Bitter sculpture, of a boy and swans, seems to have just alighted on a marble pedestal.*

OPPOSITE: *Beneath the soaring arch of a 70-foot ceiling, the Banquet Hall's magnificent appointments are worthy of a European royal palace. The rare 16th-century Flemish tapestries illustrate the lively romance of Venus and Mars and the wrath of her husband, Vulcan. The 19th-century Gothic carved thrones and the enormous table were especially designed by architect Hunt. Flags of the thirteen American colonies and the world powers at the time of Columbus, and the Vanderbilt family crest, occupy the upper reaches of the vast chamber.* LEFT: *A true country gentleman's retreat, the Billiard Room maintains a genteel masculine air with its 19th-century billiard tables and oak paneling covered with sporting and theatrical prints. Doors hidden in the fireplace wall lead to a smoking room and a gun room.*

TOP: *A wrought-iron chandelier is suspended through the center of the winding Grand Staircase.* ABOVE: *The Victorian Guest Room features 18th- and 19th-century furnishings, including an imposing German walnut tester bed and two flowered Indian prayer rugs.*

ABOVE: *The South Bedroom was Mr. Vanderbilt's; its 18th- and 19th-century Italian, Spanish and Portuguese appointments lend a Mediterranean warmth.* LEFT: *Miss Cornelia Vanderbilt's Bedroom contains a satinwood bed, marquetry wardrobe and Louis XV chaise longue.*

143

BAYOU BEND
IN TEXAS

"It is an oasis in the middle of the city," says Barry A. Greenlaw, curator of the *Bayou Bend* collection. "It is a serene, restful, rather magical place. It has an aura of graciousness." Bayou Bend, now part of the Museum of Fine Arts in Houston, Texas, is the former home of benefactress Ima Hogg and her brothers Will and Mike. The Colonial-style mansion, designed in 1927 by architect John Staub and located at the bend of Buffalo Bayou, is surrounded by towering pines and oaks. In the blooming months there are azaleas, camellias and dogwoods that fuse into the landscape like colors in an Impressionist painting. "The feeling you get from the gardens puts you in a receptive mood to visit the house," explains Mr. Greenlaw. "Miss Hogg wanted the grounds to complement the house. There are formal gardens surrounding the building, with wild gardens and woodlands intermingled. In a way, she was her own landscape architect, and she was one of the first people to bring azaleas to Houston—a remarkable feat!"

However, Miss Hogg is remembered by Texans for more than her azaleas. The daughter of James Hogg, a former governor of the state, and the granddaughter of Joseph Lewis Hogg, a member of the Congress of the Texas Republic, she accomplished a good deal in her own right. She helped found the Houston Symphony in 1913 and before her death in 1975 established a foundation for mental health at the University of Texas in Austin and the Child Guidance Center in Houston. Miss Hogg was an accomplished musician as well as a collector of art and antique furniture. She was affectionately called "Miss Ima" and the "First Lady of Texas."

"Bayou Bend, however, was never intended to be other than a home," says David Warren, senior curator of Bayou Bend and associate director of the Museum of Fine Arts. "She did entertain a great deal, particularly in conjunction with the symphony. She was apt to have small parties for the guests she had invited to a concert. She continued the practice even after she moved from Bayou Bend. But the time came when the residence was filled with American furnishings, and there wasn't a museum in Texas that could house the entire collection properly. I asked Miss Hogg if she was upset about moving out of her home. She said she was not, because she felt that, in a way, she had never owned the pieces in Bayou Bend. She was simply holding them in trust until the time came to turn them over to the people for their benefit as a cultural institution."

That day came in 1958, when the mansion was accepted as a gift by the museum. But Bayou Bend itself is seldom referred to as a museum, for Miss Hogg preferred it to be called a collection. "Bayou Bend is a reflection of Miss Hogg far more than it is a museum," says Mr. Greenlaw. "The décor is a reflection of her—not of a curator or of a committee. Her personality is reflected in the smallest details. If she liked a certain color of paint, and it was appropriate to the room, she used it whether or not the particular shade was historically accurate. And it would be a shame to change anything, for one should never lose sight of the fact that it was her vision that created Bayou Bend and her influence that makes it different from any other collection. That is the important thing."

An estimated forty thousand people tour Bayou Bend each year. "It is our aim," says the curator, "to maintain the hospitality that Miss Hogg extended to visitors. We allow only four people and one docent at a time on the tour." The experience of seeing Bayou Bend is a memorable one. As one friend of Miss Hogg said, "You leave with a sense of history. Bayou Bend and Miss Hogg are inseparable."

PRECEDING PAGE: *Bayou Bend was built in 1927 by Texas benefactress Miss Ima Hogg. Her collection spanning three centuries of American decorative arts is housed here in 24 period rooms.* BELOW: *A columned portico shades a leafy terrace on the mansion's north façade.*

RIGHT: *Hospitable surroundings make the Drawing Room, with its 18th-century furnishings, comfortable and homelike. In the foreground are graceful 1770 Newport, Rhode Island, chairs and a tea table set with English porcelain. Portraits are by Gilbert Stuart and John Wollaston; the Kirman carpet dates from circa 1800.*

OPPOSITE: *An arched entrance frames the Dining Room and its shell cupboard holding a collection of 18th-century English salt-glaze pottery. The gold-leaf wallpaper, handpainted in a flowering dogwood motif, was specially executed by William McKay for this room in 1927.* LEFT: *The warm-toned Pine Room is furnished with New England pieces, some of the William and Mary period.* ABOVE: *Colorful American glassware sparkles in a bay window. Fruits of 18th-century decorative craftsmanship include a mirror bordered in quillwork and an English stumpwork box.*

151

CHATEAU DE COPPET

Some places are endowed with an inimitable charm. They evoke the past, and with it the spirit of persons long dead who have lived in them and who have left their imprint on history. Such a place is the *Château de Coppet,* where the presence of Germaine Necker de Staël is still hauntingly felt.

In this lovely house beside Lake Geneva, the best of Europe's intelligentsia found a welcoming haven during the turbulent years of the French Revolution and the Terror that followed. Here, under the aegis of their gifted hostess, they met to exchange ideas, read their poetry and act out their dramas. Here, they flirted and quarreled. It was said that "there was more wit spent at Coppet within a single day than in the rest of the world within a whole year."

Coppet had been purchased in 1784 by Jacques Necker, a wealthy Swiss banker. Some years before Louis XVI had conferred a perilous honor upon Necker by naming him minister of finance. Thereupon, M. Necker and his wife took up residence in Paris, and it was here that their daughter Anne Louise Germaine was born and brought up. The little girl was intellectually precocious, and her mother encouraged her to develop her natural proclivities.

When the time came to seek a prestigious marriage for her, the Baron Eric Magnus de Staël-Holstein, a Swedish aristocrat attached to his country's embassy in Paris, was seeking a rich wife. Impecunious himself, he counted on an advantageous marriage as his only hope of obtaining the ambassadorship upon which he had set his heart. Germaine de Staël played her role as an ambassadress magnificently. Although not beautiful, she had a seductive charm that few could resist, and she drew around her a circle that included the most brilliant minds of the time. It was the eve of the Revolution, and Madame de Staël began to dabble in politics.

She eventually became the mistress of Louis de Narbonne, one of the last ministers of Louis XVI, and the two were soon deeply involved in plans to establish a constitutional monarchy. Threatened by the growing climate of violence in France, Germaine and her lover sought refuge in England, where Germaine's liberal views on sex and politics earned her a chilly welcome. The romance with de Narbonne soon cooled and she returned to France. There her salon flourished and she pursued her literary career.

Ever involved with men, she fell passionately in love with a charming young Swiss, Benjamin Constant. But love mixed with politics was a heady brew for the dynamic Germaine. When Napoleon came to power a few years later, she and Constant formed the center of liberal resistance to the increasingly powerful Corsican. In retaliation the First Consul forbade her to come within one hundred ten miles of Paris, the scene of her triumphs at court.

For a second time Madame de Staël went into exile, one that would last ten years. During this period she traveled extensively, but Coppet remained her headquarters. Her romance with Constant faded, to be followed by yet another. "John" Rocca, a handsome young man who was twenty-two years her junior and a member of a patrician Geneva family, fell madly in love with her. She returned his love and their liaison eventually produced a son. They later married and traveled to Sweden and then Russia. In both countries she was well received and fêted royally at court.

The arduous journeys by carriage had overtaxed her, however, and she returned to Switzerland in ill health. Within a few months she died, surrounded by her most devoted friends. She was buried in a marble tomb in the courtyard of Coppet. And here her spirit seems to live still.

When Napoleon exiled Germaine Necker de Staël from Paris, the brilliant woman-of-letters found refuge for herself and her famous salon at the Château de Coppet, near Switzerland's Lake Geneva. Built in the mid-18th century, the château had been acquired in 1784 by Mme. de Staël's father, Jacques Necker, who at one time served as Louis XVI's minister of finance. PRECEDING PAGE: A tree-filled park surrounds the château; the placid pond reflects its architectural symmetry. RIGHT, BELOW AND FAR RIGHT: A measured elegance defines the Drawing Room, where Europe's greatest minds assembled to debate political, philosophic and artistic issues. Louis XVI furniture, which dominates the room, was the height of fashion at the time. Busts of the French naturalist Buffon, portraits of Mme. de Staël's children, Imari urns and Aubusson tapestries reflect a highly selective and sparing use of decorative elements.

Likenesses of family members distinguish the
Portrait Gallery. Represented, from left to right,
are Germaine de Staël with her daughter, Alber-
tine; her son, Auguste; her father, Jacques Necker;
and Madame alone, wearing a turban.

Busts of illustrious authors surmount bookcases in the vast Library, once a gallery and the site of celebrated receptions. Here, plays by the great French tragedians — and several written by Mme. de Staël herself — were often performed.

ABOVE: *Busts of loved ones and a sensitive portrait of her closest friend, Jeanne Récamier, by Eulalie Morin, personalize Mme. de Staël's Bedroom, which is enriched by damask bed draperies, a Savonnerie rug and a mixture of striped silk wallcovering and graceful boiserie.*
OPPOSITE: *A delicately feminine Bedroom was reserved for the frequent visits of Mme. Récamier, who was known for her wit and amours. Chinese wallpaper of the period contributes to the bright and airy atmosphere.*

CREDITS

WRITERS

The following writers prepared the original
Architectural Digest articles from which the material
in this book has been adapted:

Susan Heller Anderson

Helen Barnes

James Biddle

Birgitte de Bourbon de Parme

Elizabeth Dickson

Rosemary Kent

Valentine Lawford

Gay Elliott McFarland

Wendy Murphy

Marvin D. Schwartz

Gavin Stamp

Helena Zimmerman

All original text adapted by Sam Burchell.

Caption Writers:

Joanne Jaffe

Joyce Madison

Joyce Winkel

PHOTOGRAPHERS

Alderman Studios 136-143

Robert Emmett Bright 42-51, 120-127, 152-159

Richard Champion 18-27, 28-35, 52-61, 86-95, 104-111

Chartwell National Trust of England 36-41

Alexandre Georges 144-151

Pascal Hinous 10-17, 62-67, 78-85

Countess Marie Holstein-Ledreborg 128-135

Derry Moore 96-103, 112-119

National Trust 68-77

DESIGN

Design Direction:
Philip Kaplan, Graphics Director
The Knapp Press

Book Design and Production:
Design Office/San Francisco
Bruce Kortebein
Cynthia Croker
Leigh McLellan